Y0-CZN-955

Get Up! Get Up!

Written by Honor Cline
Illustrated by Cathy Johnson

Scott Foresman

Get up! Get up!

Get up for school.

Where is a toothbrush?

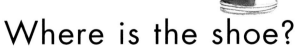

Where is the shoe?

Get up Mom!

Get up Dad!

6

Get up! Get up!

Get up for work.

But it is Saturday.

High-Frequency Words: a, the

Copyright © Pearson Education, Inc.

All Rights Reserved. Printed in the United States of America. This publication is protected by Copyright and permission should be obtained from the publisher prior to any prohibited reproduction, |storage in a retrieval system, or transmission in any form by any means, electronic, mechanical, photocopying, recording, or likewise. For information regarding permission(s), write to: Permissions Department, Scott Foresman, 1900 East Lake Avenue, Glenview, Illinois 60025.

Editorial Offices
Glenview, Illinois • Parsippany, New Jersey • New York, New York

Sales Offices
Parsippany, New Jersey • Duluth, Georgia • Glenview, Illinois
Carrollton, Texas • Ontario, California

ISBN 0-328-02269-1

5 6 7 8 9 10-V003 10 09 08 07 06

Scott Foresman Reading

Kindergarten
Independent Reader 8

High-Frequency Words:
a, the

Scott
Foresman

scottforesman.com

ISBN 0-328-02269-1

90000

9 780328 022694